MSUGH TER, M.D

Rise of the Quantum Syndicate

Copyright © 2024 by Msugh Ter, M.D

All rights reserved. No part of this publication may be reproduced, stored or transmitted in any form or by any means, electronic, mechanical, photocopying, recording, scanning, or otherwise without written permission from the publisher. It is illegal to copy this book, post it to a website, or distribute it by any other means without permission.

This novel is entirely a work of fiction. The names, characters and incidents portrayed in it are the work of the author's imagination. Any resemblance to actual persons, living or dead, events or localities is entirely coincidental.

First edition

This book was professionally typeset on Reedsy.
Find out more at reedsy.com

Contents

The Hidden Surge	1
Shadows in the Night	6
The Unseen Enemy	11
The Hidden Keys	23
The Nexus Unveiled	34
The Final Countdown	39
Secrets Beneath the Surface	44
The Hidden Vault	48
The Final Countdown	53
The Shadow's Secret	57
The Hidden Agenda	63
Dawn of a New Era	69

The Hidden Surge

Alex Reynolds stepped into the city's bustling heart, his eyes scanning the crowded streets for any sign of the strange energy readings he'd been tracking. It had been a week since he first noticed the inexplicable surges—powerful bursts of energy that seemed to ripple through the very fabric of the city. He was a young electrical engineer with a knack for finding patterns where others saw chaos. But this time, the patterns were more than just curious. They were unsettling.

The early evening sky was painted with shades of pink and orange as Alex made his way to a nondescript building on the edge of the business district. He checked his watch, noting that it was almost dusk. He had arranged to meet someone who might know more about these energy surges. The person had been vague, but Alex knew that if he was going to get to the bottom of this, he needed to follow every lead.

The building, an old warehouse that had been converted into a tech startup's office, loomed ahead. It had once been a bustling hub of activity, but now its windows were dark and its doors heavy with rust. Alex pushed open the door, and it creaked in protest. He entered cautiously, his senses on high alert. The room was dimly lit, illuminated only by the faint glow of his smartphone.

A figure emerged from the shadows. They were tall and cloaked in dark clothing, their face obscured by a hood. The figure raised a hand in a silent gesture for Alex to follow. Alex's heart raced as he followed, his footsteps echoing in the empty space.

They walked through a series of dimly lit corridors until they reached a small, locked room. The figure produced a key and opened the door, revealing a cluttered room filled with old computer equipment and mysterious gadgets. A faint hum of electronics filled the air.

"Sit," the figure instructed, pointing to a chair in front of a large computer monitor. Alex complied, his curiosity piqued.

The figure took a seat at the computer, their movements swift and practiced. They began typing rapidly, and the screen came to life with complex graphs and data. The figure's fingers danced over the keyboard as they manipulated the information, revealing a series of energy spikes mapped across the city.

"Do you know what this is?" the figure asked, their voice muffled but serious.

Alex leaned in closer, squinting at the screen. "I've been tracking these energy spikes. They're not normal. They're too powerful to be just electrical surges."

The figure nodded. "That's right. These surges are being caused by something—someone—using advanced technology or, perhaps, something even more mysterious."

Alex frowned, feeling a shiver of unease. "What do you mean, 'more mysterious'?"

The figure hesitated before speaking. "There are rumors of a secret organization—a group of people with extraordinary abilities. They've been manipulating events from behind the scenes. Some say they're responsible for these energy surges."

Alex's mind raced. He had heard whispers about superhumans in the past, but he had always dismissed them as myths or legends. Now, faced with this data and the figure's claims, he couldn't deny that something strange was happening.

"Who are they?" Alex asked. "And what do they want?"

The figure's gaze was intense. "The organization is known as the Quantum Syndicate. Their goals are unclear, but they're believed to be working to destabilize governments and control global events. They have powerful technology and, possibly, even more powerful abilities."

Alex's thoughts churned. "If they're behind these surges, then they're planning something big."

The figure nodded. "Precisely. And it's only a matter of time before they make their move. That's why you're here. We need to gather more information and find out what they're planning before it's too late."

Alex's resolve hardened. "I'm in. What do we need to do?"

The figure slid a folder across the table. "This contains everything we know about the Quantum Syndicate so far. It's not much, but it's a start. You'll need to dig deeper, gather evidence, and find out how they're operating."

Alex took the folder and opened it. Inside were documents, photos, and notes—some of which were incomplete or cryptic. He skimmed through them, trying to piece together the puzzle.

"I'll start right away," Alex said, determination in his voice. "But I need to know more about you. Who are you, and why are you helping me?"

The figure's hooded head lowered slightly. "My name is Samara. I was once part of the Syndicate, but I left when I realized their true intentions. Now,

I'm working to stop them from causing further harm."

Alex looked at Samara, trying to read her expression through the shadows of her hood. "How can I trust you?"

Samara's voice softened. "You have no reason to trust me completely, but time is of the essence. If we don't act now, the Syndicate's plans could cause untold damage. We need to work together to prevent that."

Alex took a deep breath and nodded. "Alright. I'll do my best."

Samara handed him a small device. "This is a tracker. It will help us monitor any unusual activity related to the energy surges. Keep it with you at all times."

Alex examined the device, noting its sleek design and advanced technology. He slipped it into his pocket, feeling its weight and significance.

With a final nod, Samara turned and walked toward the door. "I'll be in touch with more information. Stay vigilant, Alex. The Syndicate is more dangerous than you can imagine."

Alex watched as Samara disappeared into the shadows, leaving him alone in the dimly lit room. He glanced at the folder and then at the tracker in his pocket. His mind buzzed with questions and possibilities. He knew he was stepping into a world of danger and intrigue, but he was determined to uncover the truth and stop whatever the Quantum Syndicate had planned.

As he left the building and stepped out into the cool evening air, Alex felt a mix of excitement and apprehension. The city around him seemed unchanged, but he knew that beneath its surface, a hidden conflict was brewing—one that would test his skills, challenge his beliefs, and reveal secrets he had never imagined.

With renewed purpose, Alex set off into the night, ready to face whatever lay ahead and uncover the mysteries of the Quantum Syndicate.

Shadows in the Night

The night had fallen heavy over the city, casting long shadows that danced under the streetlights. Alex Reynolds walked briskly through the darkened streets, his mind racing with thoughts of the Quantum Syndicate. The folder Samara had given him was clutched tightly in his hand, and the small device she had handed him was tucked safely in his pocket. The city's usual hum of activity seemed to be muffled by the weight of the night.

Alex's apartment was a short walk from the warehouse, but he decided to take a longer route, wanting to clear his head before diving into the mysterious documents. He walked past familiar landmarks—places he had seen a thousand times, but now they seemed different, almost foreboding. His eyes kept darting to every shadow, every flicker of movement.

As he neared his building, Alex felt a chill creep up his spine. The sense of being watched was growing stronger. He quickened his pace, his heartbeat echoing in his ears. When he reached his apartment door, he glanced around one last time before quickly unlocking it and slipping inside.

The apartment was small but comfortable, cluttered with the usual assortment of books, electronics, and the remnants of takeout meals. Alex took a deep breath and settled at his desk. He set the folder down and pulled out a lamp, casting a warm light over his workspace. His first priority was to sort through the documents and see if he could find any clues about the Quantum Syndicate.

He opened the folder and began sorting through the papers. There were maps of the city with strange symbols marked on them, photos of people whose faces were blurred or obscured, and notes written in hurried, sometimes illegible handwriting. Alex picked up a photograph of a tall, imposing building with a large, dark symbol painted on the side. The building was marked on one of the maps.

Alex studied the map closely. The symbol on the building matched a symbol he had seen earlier in the documents. His attention was drawn to a small note scribbled in the margin: "The Nexus—heart of the Syndicate." The Nexus. Alex's heart raced. This was the first concrete lead he had found.

He decided to investigate the building marked as the Nexus. According to the map, it was located in a more secluded part of town, away from the busy streets and hidden among old warehouses and abandoned lots. Alex made a plan to visit the location early the next morning before anyone was around.

After setting aside the documents for later, Alex felt exhaustion tugging at him. He decided to get some rest, knowing he would need all his energy for the investigation ahead. As he lay in bed, sleep came slowly, his mind buzzing with the day's revelations.

The next morning, Alex awoke with the first light of dawn. He quickly dressed and grabbed his backpack, stuffing the folder inside along with a flashlight and some basic tools. He knew he would need to be cautious—if the Nexus was as important as the documents suggested, it would likely be guarded.

He left his apartment and made his way to the Nexus. The sun was barely up, casting long shadows across the city. The streets were quiet, and a light fog hung in the air, adding to the eerie atmosphere. As Alex approached the building, he could see it looming in the distance—a dark, imposing structure with a foreboding presence.

The Nexus was surrounded by a high fence with barbed wire at the top. The building itself was old and decrepit, with broken windows and faded paint. Alex could see a small gate in the fence, partially hidden by overgrown shrubs. He approached the gate and found it unlocked. With a quick glance around, he slipped through and made his way to the building.

The front entrance was boarded up, but Alex noticed a small side door that was slightly ajar. He approached cautiously, his senses on high alert. He eased the door open and slipped inside, his flashlight casting a beam of light into the darkness.

The interior of the Nexus was just as grim as the outside. Dust covered everything, and the air was thick with the smell of decay. Alex moved carefully through the building, his footsteps echoing in the empty halls. He was looking for anything that might give him more information about the Quantum Syndicate.

He explored several rooms, each one filled with old furniture and forgotten objects. In one room, he found a set of old computers, their screens cracked and covered in dust. He tried turning one on, but it was dead. He moved on, hoping to find something more useful.

In the far corner of the building, Alex stumbled upon a staircase leading down to a basement. His flashlight illuminated the steps as he descended slowly, each step creaking under his weight. The basement was cold and damp, with a faint smell of mildew.

At the bottom of the stairs, Alex found a large door, slightly ajar. He pushed it open and stepped inside. The room was filled with strange equipment—machines and devices that Alex didn't recognize. On one side of the room, there was a large table covered in blueprints and documents.

Alex approached the table and began examining the papers. The blueprints detailed various parts of the Nexus, including secret rooms and hidden passages. There were also documents related to advanced technology and energy manipulation. Alex's eyes widened as he realized that this was the heart of the Syndicate's operations.

He began taking photos of the documents with his phone, trying to capture as much information as possible. Suddenly, he heard a noise—a faint sound of footsteps coming from upstairs. His heart skipped a beat. Someone was coming.

Alex quickly grabbed the folder and documents, shoving them into his backpack. He turned off his flashlight and slipped into a shadowy corner of the room, hoping he wouldn't be seen. The footsteps grew louder, and Alex could hear voices speaking in hushed tones.

He held his breath as the door to the basement creaked open. Two figures entered the room, their faces obscured by masks. They moved with purpose, examining the equipment and discussing something in low voices. Alex could only make out fragments of their conversation.

"… The extraction is set for tonight. We need to be ready…" one of them said.

Alex strained to hear more but couldn't catch any details. He knew he had to leave before he was discovered. He waited until the figures were engrossed in their work, then quietly slipped out of the room and back up the stairs.

As he reached the main floor, he glanced back and saw that the basement door was still open. He made his way back to the side door and slipped outside, retracing his steps through the overgrown shrubs and out of the fenced area.

Once he was safely on the street, Alex took a deep breath and tried to calm his racing heart. He needed to process what he had seen and figure out his next move. He headed back to his apartment, his mind filled with questions and concerns.

The documents he had taken from the Nexus were filled with detailed plans and blueprints. There were also references to an "extraction" planned for that night. Alex knew he had to act quickly to uncover what the Syndicate was planning and to stop them if he could.

As he reached his apartment, Alex took one last look at the documents before sitting down at his desk. The pieces of the puzzle were starting to come together, but he still had a lot to learn. He needed to find out what the extraction was and how it fit into the Syndicate's larger plans.

With renewed determination, Alex began to sift through the documents, piecing together the information he had gathered. He knew that the stakes were high, and he couldn't afford to make any mistakes. The Quantum Syndicate was a powerful and dangerous enemy, and he was only beginning to understand the full scope of their plans.

As the sun began to set, casting long shadows across the city, Alex felt a sense of urgency. The Syndicate's plans were unfolding, and he needed to stay ahead of them. He was determined to uncover the truth and stop whatever threat the Syndicate posed.

With the documents spread out before him, Alex continued his investigation, driven by a sense of purpose and a desire to protect the city from the shadows lurking within it.

The Unseen Enemy

The sun was just starting to rise when Alex Reynolds woke up. His sleep had been restless, filled with dreams of shadowy figures and mysterious devices. He rubbed his eyes and stretched, trying to shake off the lingering sense of unease. Today was going to be crucial. He had to figure out what the Quantum Syndicate was planning and stop them before it was too late.

He sat at his desk, surrounded by the documents he had taken from the Nexus. The blueprints and plans were detailed, showing various rooms and hidden passages within the Nexus. One document stood out—a list of names and dates that seemed to reference important events and people.

Alex focused on this document, hoping it might give him more clues. He noticed a series of dates marked with red circles. One date, in particular, stood out: "Tonight—Operation Eclipse." It was clear that something significant was planned for tonight, and Alex had to find out what it was.

He pulled out his phone and started searching for any events or activities happening in the city tonight. After some digging, he found a charity gala taking place at an upscale hotel. The timing seemed suspiciously perfect—it was the same night as the "Operation Eclipse." He decided to investigate further.

Alex dressed quickly, opting for a suit to blend in at the gala. He wasn't sure if this event was directly related to the Syndicate's plan, but he had to start somewhere. He hoped that the gala, with its high-profile guests and security, might provide some answers.

He arrived at the hotel just before the gala was set to begin. The grand entrance was lined with elegant cars, and guests in formal attire were arriving in droves. Alex took a deep breath and joined the stream of people, trying to appear as inconspicuous as possible. He showed his invitation at the door and was ushered into the lavishly decorated ballroom.

Inside, the room was filled with glittering chandeliers, elaborate floral arrangements, and a band playing soft, classical music. The guests mingled, enjoying cocktails and hors d'oeuvres. Alex scanned the room, looking for anything that might connect to the Quantum Syndicate.

He noticed a group of guests who seemed unusually tense, whispering to each other and glancing around nervously. They were dressed in expensive suits and gowns, standing near a corner of the room where a large, ornate safe was displayed. The safe was part of the gala's silent auction, but something about it caught Alex's attention.

He approached the group casually, pretending to be interested in the auction items. As he got closer, he overheard snippets of their conversation.

"Tonight is the night," one of them said in a hushed tone. "The extraction needs to go off without a hitch."

Alex's heart raced. It was clear that these people were talking about something important. He tried to get closer to hear more, but just then, a waiter bumped into him, spilling a drink on his suit. Alex apologized and took a step back, trying to regain his composure.

He needed to find a way to get closer to the safe and see if there was anything inside it. Alex noticed a service door at the far end of the room, slightly ajar.

He made his way towards it, slipping through and finding himself in a small, dimly lit hallway.

He walked quietly down the hallway, listening for any sounds. He reached a door labeled "Storage" and opened it carefully. Inside, he found a small room filled with boxes and supplies. He searched through the boxes, hoping to find something useful. In one of the boxes, he found a set of keys and a note with instructions.

The note read: "Unlock the safe and retrieve the package. Be discreet. The extraction is crucial."

Alex's mind raced. The package in the safe must be part of the Syndicate's plan. He took the keys and headed back to the ballroom, trying to stay calm. He approached the safe, glancing around to make sure no one was watching.

He inserted the key into the lock and turned it slowly. The safe clicked open, and Alex's heart pounded as he opened the door. Inside, there was a small, black briefcase. He quickly closed the safe and took the briefcase, slipping it into his backpack.

As he was about to leave, he heard footsteps approaching. Alex hurried back to the service door and slipped through just in time to see a group of men in dark suits entering the storage room. He hid behind a stack of boxes, holding his breath.

The men started talking, their voices low and urgent. "The package is in the safe," one of them said. "We need to make sure it gets to the extraction point."

Alex's mind was racing. He had to figure out where the extraction point was. He waited until the men left the room, then slipped out and made his way back to the ballroom.

He decided to follow the group of guests he had overheard earlier. They were making their way towards a side exit, and Alex followed discreetly. They led him to a private area of the hotel, where a small, nondescript van was parked.

The group gathered around the van, talking in low voices. Alex hid behind a nearby pillar, trying to catch as much information as he could. He saw them loading the briefcase into the van, along with several other items.

One of the men opened a laptop and began typing quickly. Alex glanced at the screen from his hiding spot and saw a map of the city with several locations marked. One location was labeled "Operation Eclipse—Final Stage."

Alex's heart raced. He had to get to this location before it was too late. He waited until the group was busy with their preparations, then made his way to the van. He managed to slip into the back without being noticed, hiding among the boxes and equipment.

The van started moving, and Alex felt a sense of relief mixed with anxiety. He had to stay hidden until they reached their destination. The ride was long and filled with the rumble of the engine and the occasional conversation between the men in the front.

Eventually, the van came to a stop. Alex listened carefully and heard the sound of the van doors opening. He waited until the men had started unloading the items, then slipped out of the van and into the shadows.

He found himself in a secluded industrial area on the outskirts of town. The buildings were old and rundown, and there were few lights. Alex followed the men at a distance, staying hidden behind crates and barrels.

The group moved towards a large, fortified warehouse. There were guards stationed outside, and the area was heavily secured. Alex knew he had to be careful. He watched as the men entered the warehouse, their voices fading as they went inside.

Alex took a deep breath and approached the warehouse, looking for a way in. He found a small, broken window on the side of the building and managed to squeeze through. Inside, the warehouse was dark and filled with the sounds of machinery.

He crept through the shadows, following the sounds of voices. He finally reached a large, central room where the group was gathered. The room was filled with high-tech equipment and computers, and in the center was a large container.

The briefcase was being opened, and the contents were revealed. Alex could see a strange device, glowing with an eerie light. The men were talking excitedly about the device and its capabilities.

"We've finally got it," one of them said. "With this, we can control the energy surges and execute the extraction as planned."

Alex's mind raced. This device must be what the Syndicate was after. He needed to find a way to stop them before they could use it. He looked around for anything he could use to disrupt their plans.

He spotted a large control panel on the side of the room. It had several buttons and switches, and it looked like it controlled the warehouse's systems. Alex quickly made his way over to it, trying to figure out how it worked.

As he was working on the control panel, he heard footsteps approaching. He glanced back and saw a guard walking towards him. Panicking, Alex grabbed a wrench from a nearby toolbox and ducked behind a stack of crates.

The guard entered the room and began searching. Alex held his breath, trying to stay as quiet as possible. The guard's footsteps grew closer, and Alex prepared to act if necessary.

Just as the guard was about to discover him, he heard a loud noise from the other side of the room. The distraction caused the guard to turn his attention away, giving Alex a chance to slip past and hide behind a nearby stack of equipment.

Alex continued working on the control panel, his fingers moving quickly over the buttons and switches. He managed to shut down several systems, causing alarms to go off and lights to flash. The chaos caused the Syndicate members to scramble, giving Alex the perfect opportunity to make his move.

He grabbed the strange device from the center of the room and started to leave. As he made his way back to the broken window, he heard shouting and commotion behind him. The guards were mobilizing, and it was clear that he needed to leave quickly.

Alex climbed through the window and made his way back into the night. He ran through the industrial area, his heart pounding with adrenaline. He knew he had to get back to his apartment and analyze the device to understand its purpose and how to stop it.

As he reached his apartment, Alex took a deep breath and closed the door behind him. He set the device on his desk and began examining it. The device was intricate, with glowing symbols and circuits that seemed to pulse with energy.

He needed to figure out how it worked and what the Syndicate planned to do with it. He knew that time was running out, and he had to act fast to prevent any further danger.

With determination, Alex set to work, ready to uncover the secrets of the device and stop the Quantum Syndicate's plans before it was too late.

As Alex examined the device, he noticed that it had a series of symbols and connections that looked like they were meant to interface with other technology. The glowing symbols were unlike anything he had seen before, pulsating in a rhythmic pattern. He carefully took out his toolkit and began to examine the internal components.

The device had several small panels that could be opened. Alex pried one open and saw a tangle of wires and circuits. He started to trace the connections, trying to understand how the device worked. It was clear that this was more than just a simple gadget—it was a piece of advanced technology with a complex design.

He continued working on the device, noting the patterns and connections. It became evident that the device was designed to manipulate energy in some way. The symbols on it seemed to correspond to different types of energy, suggesting that it could control or alter various energy fields.

As he worked, Alex's thoughts kept drifting back to the Syndicate's plans. They had mentioned an "extraction," and this device seemed to be a key component. He needed to understand how it fit into their overall scheme.

Hours passed as Alex delved deeper into the device. He used his laptop to cross-reference the symbols and patterns with the information he had gathered. He found some similarities between the device's symbols and ancient alchemical symbols, which suggested that the device might be based on old, forgotten knowledge.

Just as Alex was about to make a breakthrough, he heard a knock at his door. He froze, his heart racing. Who could it be at this hour? He grabbed the device and hid it quickly in a drawer before cautiously approaching the door.

He peered through the peephole and saw a familiar face—Samara, the woman who had given him the folder. She looked anxious and determined. Alex hesitated for a moment before opening the door.

"Samara, what are you doing here?" he asked, trying to keep his voice steady.

"We don't have much time," Samara said, stepping inside quickly. "The Syndicate is moving faster than we anticipated. I came to check on you and see if you've found anything."

Alex nodded and led her to his desk, where he pulled out the documents and showed her the information he had uncovered. Samara's eyes widened as she looked at the device.

"This is worse than I thought," she said, her voice filled with concern. "The Syndicate's plans are more dangerous than we realized. This device can manipulate energy on a massive scale. If they use it as planned, they could cause widespread destruction."

Alex's heart sank. He had suspected that the device was powerful, but he hadn't realized the full extent of its potential for harm. "What do we do?" he asked. "How can we stop them?"

"We need to find out where they are planning to use the device," Samara said. "The extraction point you saw on the map—do you know where it is?"

Alex nodded. "I saw it marked as 'Operation Eclipse—Final Stage.' I think it's in an old factory on the outskirts of town."

"That's where we need to go," Samara said. "We have to get there before they activate the device."

Alex and Samara gathered their things quickly, taking the device and the documents with them. They decided to drive to the old factory, hoping to arrive before the Syndicate's operation began. The drive was tense, with both of them lost in their thoughts, the weight of the situation heavy on their minds.

As they approached the factory, Alex noticed that the area was heavily guarded. There were security cameras and guards stationed around the perimeter. The factory itself was an imposing structure, with tall, barbed-wire fences and large, dark windows.

Alex and Samara parked a few blocks away and approached the factory on foot, sticking to the shadows to avoid being seen. They found a spot where they could observe the entrance and the guards. Samara pulled out a small device and began scanning the area for any weak spots in the security.

After a few minutes, she looked up and said, "There's a small maintenance door around the back that looks like it might be less guarded. We could use that to get inside."

Alex nodded, and they carefully made their way to the back of the factory. They approached the maintenance door and found it unlocked. Samara pushed it open quietly, and they slipped inside.

The interior of the factory was dark and filled with the sounds of machinery. The air was thick with dust, and the floor was littered with debris. Alex and Samara moved cautiously through the building, their footsteps echoing in the silence.

They followed the signs and blueprints from the documents, heading towards the central area of the factory. The device they had seen earlier was likely the key to the Syndicate's plans, and they needed to find it before it was too late.

As they moved deeper into the factory, they encountered several guards patrolling the area. Alex and Samara managed to avoid detection by hiding behind crates and machinery. They continued on, their nerves on edge as they approached the main control room.

When they reached the control room, they found it heavily guarded. There were several guards stationed outside, and the door was locked. Alex and Samara exchanged worried glances. They needed to find another way in.

Samara pulled out a small, portable lock-picking tool and began working on the lock. It took a few minutes, but she managed to get it open. They slipped inside and found themselves in a room filled with high-tech equipment and monitors.

In the center of the room was the strange device they had seen earlier. It was connected to a large machine with numerous cables and wires. The machine was humming with energy, and the device was glowing with an eerie light.

"This is it," Samara said, her voice filled with determination. "We need to disable the device and shut down the machine."

Alex nodded and moved towards the control panel, trying to figure out how to stop the machine. He noticed a series of switches and buttons, each one labeled with various functions. He began pressing buttons and flipping switches, trying to deactivate the machine.

As he worked, he heard footsteps approaching. The guards were coming closer, and Alex knew they didn't have much time. He worked quickly, his heart racing as he tried to disable the machine.

Samara kept watch, ready to alert Alex if the guards got too close. The tension in the room was palpable as Alex continued working on the controls. He could see the device's energy levels dropping as he disabled the machine, but there were still some systems that needed to be shut down.

Just as he was about to finish, the door to the control room burst open, and a group of Syndicate members stormed in. They were armed and looked furious.

"Stop them!" one of them shouted. "They're trying to sabotage the operation!"

Alex and Samara quickly sprang into action. They grabbed whatever tools and equipment they could find and prepared to defend themselves. The Syndicate members moved towards them, their faces masked with anger and determination.

A fight broke out, with Alex and Samara doing their best to hold off the attackers. Alex swung a wrench at one of the Syndicate members, while Samara used a nearby pipe as a makeshift weapon. The room was filled with the sounds of clashing metal and shouts.

Despite their efforts, the Syndicate members were relentless. Alex could see that they were running out of time. He needed to finish disabling the machine before it was too late.

With a final effort, Alex managed to shut down the last of the machine's systems. The glowing device flickered and dimmed, its energy levels dropping to zero. The Syndicate members seemed to realize that their plans were being thwarted, and their anger grew.

Alex and Samara fought bravely, but they were outnumbered. They managed to hold off the attackers long enough to make a hasty escape. They ran through the factory, dodging guards and avoiding traps.

Finally, they made it back to the maintenance door and out into the night. They were breathless and bruised, but they had successfully stopped the Syndicate's operation. The device was no longer a threat, and the machine had been disabled.

As they walked away from the factory, Alex and Samara took a moment to catch their breath. The city was quiet, and the first light of dawn was beginning to appear on the horizon.

"We did it," Samara said, her voice filled with relief. "We stopped them."

Alex nodded, feeling a sense of accomplishment mixed with exhaustion. "But we need to stay vigilant. The Syndicate won't give up easily."

They both knew that their fight was far from over. The Quantum Syndicate was a powerful and dangerous enemy, and there would be more challenges ahead. But for now, they had made a significant victory.

As they made their way back to their safehouse, Alex and Samara were determined to keep fighting. They had uncovered part of the Syndicate's plan and stopped a major threat, but the battle was far from over. They would continue to uncover the secrets of the Quantum Syndicate and protect the city from the shadows lurking within it.

The Hidden Keys

Alex and Samara had spent the night recovering from their escape. They needed to regroup and plan their next move. The early morning sun peeked through the curtains of their safehouse, casting a soft light over the room.

Alex sat at the kitchen table, examining the strange device they had taken from the factory. Samara was making coffee, her hands moving quickly as she prepared the morning brew. The events of the previous night had left them both tired, but there was no time to rest. They needed to understand the device and figure out their next steps.

"Do you have any idea what this device does?" Samara asked as she set a steaming cup of coffee in front of Alex.

Alex shook his head. "Not yet. I've been looking at the symbols and the circuits, but I haven't figured out how it works. It seems to be some kind of energy manipulator, but its exact purpose is still unclear."

Samara took a sip of her coffee and nodded. "We need to find more information. If the Syndicate wanted it so badly, it must be important."

Alex agreed. He pulled out the documents they had taken from the Nexus and began sorting through them. Among the papers was a map with several locations marked. One of the locations was a library downtown, labeled "Research and Archives."

"Maybe the library has more information about this device," Alex suggested. "If we can find records or old manuscripts, we might learn more about its purpose."

Samara nodded in agreement. "Let's check it out. We need all the information we can get."

They finished their coffee and set out for the library. The downtown area was bustling with activity as they made their way through the crowded streets. The library was a large, old building with tall columns and an impressive facade. It looked like a place where they might find valuable information.

Inside, the library was quiet and cool. Rows of bookshelves stretched out before them, filled with volumes of every size and shape. Alex and Samara headed towards the research and archives section, hoping to find something useful.

The archives were located in a separate, enclosed room at the back of the library. It was filled with old books, manuscripts, and documents. A librarian sat at a desk near the entrance, watching as Alex and Samara entered.

"Can I help you with anything?" the librarian asked.

Alex stepped forward. "We're looking for information on ancient devices and energy manipulation. We've come across a strange device, and we're hoping to find any historical records or manuscripts that might shed light on its purpose."

The librarian raised an eyebrow but nodded. "We have some old manuscripts on that subject. I'll show you where to find them."

The librarian led them to a set of shelves filled with ancient books and scrolls. Alex and Samara began examining the materials, looking for anything that might be relevant. They pulled out several manuscripts and began reading through them.

Hours passed as they sifted through the old texts. Many of the manuscripts were written in dense, archaic language, making them difficult to understand. But after a while, Samara came across a book with a familiar symbol on the cover—the same symbol that was on the device.

"Alex, look at this," Samara said, pointing to the book. "This symbol matches the one on the device."

Alex took the book and began flipping through the pages. The text was old and worn, but he could make out some important details. The book described an ancient form of energy manipulation used in old alchemical practices. It mentioned devices that could control and harness energy for various purposes.

"This book might be exactly what we need," Alex said. "It talks about energy manipulation and ancient devices. We might find some clues about how the device works and what the Syndicate plans to do with it."

Samara nodded. "Let's take some notes and see if we can piece together the information."

They spent the next few hours taking detailed notes from the book. They found references to several ancient devices used for different purposes, including energy control and amplification. Some of the devices were described as having the ability to channel energy into powerful bursts, while others could stabilize or redirect energy flows.

As they worked, Alex's phone buzzed with a message. It was from a contact he had in law enforcement, asking for a meeting. The message mentioned something about a break in the case they were working on.

"We should check this out," Samara suggested. "If the police have new information, it might help us understand what's happening."

They packed up their notes and headed to the meeting location, which was a small police station on the outskirts of town. The building was modest, but the officers inside were busy with their work.

Alex and Samara met with Detective Riley, a no-nonsense investigator who had been helping them behind the scenes. Riley was waiting for them in his office, looking serious.

"Glad you could make it," Riley said. "We've got some new leads on the Syndicate. We've been tracking their activities, and it looks like they're planning something big."

Alex and Samara took a seat and listened as Riley outlined the new information. The police had found evidence of a large shipment of equipment being delivered to a remote location outside the city. The shipment included several high-tech devices, similar to the one Alex and Samara had encountered.

"We believe the Syndicate is setting up a new operation," Riley explained. "We don't know exactly what they're planning, but it's likely related to the device you found."

Alex nodded, his mind racing. "We need to find out more about this location. If they're setting up something new, it could be connected to their plans."

Riley agreed. "I'll provide you with the address of the location and any relevant information we have. But be careful—this operation might be heavily guarded."

They left the police station with the new information and headed back to their safehouse. They had the address of the remote location and knew that they needed to investigate further.

As they prepared for their next move, Alex and Samara reviewed the notes from the library. The book had provided valuable insights into the device's purpose and how it could be used. They found references to a "key" that was needed to activate the device fully. The key was described as an ancient artifact that could control the device's energy output.

"We need to find this key," Samara said. "If the Syndicate has it, it means they have the means to use the device to its full potential."

Alex agreed. "We need to find out where the key is and how we can get it before the Syndicate does."

They decided to focus on finding the key and understanding its connection to the device. The remote location mentioned by the police might hold more clues or be part of the Syndicate's plan.

The following day, Alex and Samara set out for the remote location. It was a long drive through winding roads and dense forests. As they approached, they saw a large, fenced-in area with security cameras and guards.

They parked a safe distance away and observed the site. It was a high-tech facility with several buildings and equipment scattered around. It looked like a research and development center.

Alex and Samara carefully approached the facility, using the cover of the trees and shadows to stay hidden. They found a small, less guarded entry point and slipped inside. The area was filled with various machinery and equipment, much of it similar to what they had seen at the factory.

They moved cautiously through the facility, looking for any signs of the key or additional information. They came across a large storage room filled with crates and boxes. Alex and Samara began searching through the crates, hoping to find something useful.

After some time, Samara discovered a locked cabinet in the corner of the room. The cabinet had a label that read "Artifact Storage." Alex took out his tools and worked on the lock, trying to open it without drawing attention.

With a click, the lock gave way, and Alex opened the cabinet. Inside, they found several old, dusty artifacts and boxes. One of the boxes had an inscription that matched the description of the key they had read about in the book.

"This might be it," Alex said, carefully opening the box. Inside, he found an ancient-looking artifact with intricate designs and symbols. The artifact seemed to emit a faint, pulsating light.

Samara examined the artifact closely. "This could be the key we've been looking for. We need to get it back and see if it fits with the device."

They carefully packed the artifact and left the facility, making their way back to their safehouse. The drive was tense, with both of them focused on the importance of their find.

Once back at the safehouse, Alex and Samara took the artifact to their study area. They carefully examined it, comparing it to the device. The symbols and designs on the artifact matched some of the symbols on the device.

"It looks like this artifact is designed to work with the device," Alex said. "We need to test it and see if it activates the device."

They set up the device and the artifact on a table and began their test. Alex carefully placed the artifact in a specific slot on the device, as described in the notes they had taken from the library.

As the artifact was inserted, the device started to hum and glow with a bright light. The energy readings on the device began to stabilize, and the previously erratic pulses became steady and controlled.

"This is incredible," Samara said, her eyes wide with amazement. "The artifact is definitely linked to the device."

With the artifact in place, the device seemed to be functioning as intended. The energy levels were consistent, and the device was no longer a threat. Alex and Samara had successfully activated the device and ensured that it was under control.

They knew, however, that their work was not done. The Syndicate would likely be planning to reclaim the artifact and continue their plans. Alex and Samara needed to stay ahead of them.

With the device now functioning correctly, Alex and Samara began preparing for their next steps. They decided to study the artifact and the device more closely to understand their full capabilities and limitations. If the Syndicate had plans to use this technology for nefarious purposes, they needed to be ready.

As they worked, Samara looked over their notes and documents, piecing together the information they had gathered. She came across a reference in one of the old manuscripts about a "control center" used to monitor and manage energy devices. This center was described as a hidden facility where energy manipulation technology was developed and controlled.

"This control center might be where the Syndicate is planning their next move," Samara suggested. "If they're using this device, they might have a central location where they oversee their operations."

Alex agreed. "We should find out more about this control center. It could lead us to the Syndicate's main operation and help us stop them before it's too late."

They researched the location mentioned in the manuscript and found a possible site that matched the description. It was an abandoned warehouse on the outskirts of the city, known for its secrecy and lack of public information. This site seemed like a plausible location for the Syndicate's control center.

The next day, Alex and Samara set out for the warehouse. The area was isolated, with few buildings around and a sense of quiet that contrasted with the bustling city they had just left. The warehouse was large and dilapidated, with broken windows and rusted doors.

They approached the building cautiously, using the cover of the surrounding trees and shadows. Alex spotted a side entrance that was partially open, allowing them to slip inside without drawing attention.

The interior of the warehouse was dark and filled with old equipment and debris. They moved quietly through the building, their footsteps muffled by the thick layer of dust on the floor. Alex and Samara used their flashlights to illuminate their path, searching for any signs of activity or clues.

As they explored, they found a set of stairs leading down to a basement level. The stairs creaked under their weight, but they continued downward, determined to find the control center.

The basement was a stark contrast to the rest of the warehouse. It was filled with high-tech equipment, computers, and control panels. The room was well-lit and appeared to be operational, suggesting that it was currently in use.

Alex and Samara carefully moved through the control center, avoiding the areas where guards were patrolling. They saw several screens displaying surveillance footage and data about energy levels, indicating that the Syndicate was closely monitoring their operations.

They approached one of the control panels and began examining the data. The screens showed various locations and activities, including details about the device they had found. It was clear that the Syndicate was using this control center to manage their plans and track their technology.

"This is it," Samara said. "We need to gather as much information as we can before we leave. This control center is the heart of their operations."

Alex nodded and started copying the data from the control panels onto a portable drive. He was careful to ensure that they did not trigger any alarms or alert the Syndicate to their presence. Samara kept watch, her eyes scanning the area for any approaching guards.

As they worked, Alex noticed a set of blueprints on a desk. The blueprints detailed several key locations and facilities, including a new site where the Syndicate planned to test and deploy their energy devices. The site was marked as "Project Nexus—Phase 2."

"We need to get these blueprints," Alex said. "They might give us crucial information about the Syndicate's next steps."

They quickly copied the blueprints and finished gathering the data from the control panels. With their mission accomplished, they made their way back to the stairs and headed out of the control center.

As they exited the warehouse, Alex and Samara were relieved to have avoided detection. They made their way back to their safehouse, eager to review the information they had collected.

Back at the safehouse, Alex and Samara began analyzing the data and blueprints. The information revealed that the Syndicate's next phase involved deploying their energy technology on a large scale. They planned to use the devices to control and manipulate energy across the city, potentially causing widespread disruptions.

"We need to stop them before they can execute their plans," Samara said. "If they succeed, it could have disastrous consequences for the entire city."

Alex agreed. "We need to find the location of their next operation and come up with a plan to neutralize their technology. We also need to ensure that the device and artifact remain secure."

They spent the night planning their next move. They reviewed the blueprints and identified key locations where the Syndicate might be setting up their equipment. They also made arrangements to secure the device and artifact, ensuring that they remained out of the Syndicate's reach.

The following day, Alex and Samara set out to investigate the locations identified in the blueprints. They visited several sites, gathering more information and confirming the Syndicate's plans. Each location they visited brought them closer to understanding the full scope of the Syndicate's operation.

Their investigation revealed that the Syndicate was planning to deploy their technology in several critical areas, including power grids and communication networks. The scale of their operation was larger than they had anticipated, and the potential impact was significant.

"We have to act fast," Alex said. "If we can disrupt their plans and neutralize their technology, we might be able to prevent them from causing major disruptions."

They formulated a plan to target key locations and sabotage the Syndicate's equipment. They also reached out to their contacts for additional support, coordinating with law enforcement and other allies to ensure that they had the resources they needed.

As the day of the Syndicate's planned operation approached, Alex and Samara prepared for their final confrontation. They knew that the stakes were high and that they needed to be ready for anything.

With their plan in place, they set out to execute their mission. The city was on edge as they worked to disrupt the Syndicate's plans and protect the people from the impending threat. The outcome of their efforts would determine whether they could stop the Syndicate and ensure the safety of the city.

The battle was far from over, but Alex and Samara were determined to see it through. They had faced many challenges and dangers, but their resolve remained strong. They were ready to confront the Syndicate and put an end to their plans once and for all.

The Nexus Unveiled

The city buzzed with activity as Alex and Samara prepared for their final confrontation with the Syndicate. The stakes were high, and they knew that time was running out. Their plan was to disrupt the Syndicate's operation and stop them from deploying their dangerous technology.

Early in the morning, Alex and Samara reviewed their strategy. They had identified several key locations where the Syndicate was setting up their equipment. Their goal was to reach these sites before the Syndicate could activate their devices and cause chaos.

The first location on their list was a power station on the edge of the city. This site was crucial because the Syndicate planned to use it to manipulate the city's power grid. Alex and Samara knew that they needed to act quickly to prevent any disruptions.

They drove to the power station, taking a route that avoided main roads and potential checkpoints. The power station was a large facility surrounded by fences and security cameras. They parked their car at a distance and approached on foot, using the cover of early morning fog to stay hidden.

As they neared the facility, Alex spotted a small maintenance door at the back of the building. It was slightly ajar, likely left open by workers or guards. They carefully slipped through the door and into the station.

Inside, the power station was a maze of equipment and control panels. The walls were lined with large machines and monitors displaying real-time data about the power grid. Alex and Samara moved stealthily, making their way to the control room where the Syndicate's devices were being set up.

The control room was guarded by two security personnel. Alex and Samara waited for the right moment, watching the guards from a hidden vantage point. When the guards turned their backs, Alex signaled to Samara. They moved quickly, slipping into the control room and disabling the guards before they could react.

With the guards out of the way, Alex and Samara examined the equipment. The Syndicate's devices were connected to the power grid, and they were set to activate soon. Alex began disconnecting the devices while Samara kept watch for any signs of trouble.

As Alex worked, he noticed that the devices were rigged with advanced security measures. He had to be careful not to trigger any alarms or alerts. He used his tools to carefully dismantle the devices and remove their power sources.

Meanwhile, Samara scanned the control room for any additional information. She found a terminal with access to the power grid's control system. She quickly accessed the system and checked for any signs of tampering or unauthorized activity.

"It looks like the Syndicate has been setting up their equipment to override the power grid's controls," Samara said. "We need to make sure that their changes are reversed before we leave."

Alex finished disabling the devices and joined Samara at the terminal. Together, they worked to undo the Syndicate's changes and restore the power grid to its normal state. It took some time, but they managed to reverse the modifications and secure the power station.

With the power station secured, they left the facility and drove to the next location on their list—a communications tower in a remote area. The tower was essential for the Syndicate's plans because it would allow them to disrupt communication networks across the city.

The communications tower was a tall, imposing structure surrounded by a chain-link fence. There were several guards patrolling the area, and Alex and Samara had to be careful to avoid detection.

They approached the tower under the cover of darkness, using the shadows to stay hidden. Alex noticed a small maintenance hatch at the base of the tower. They carefully opened it and climbed inside, making their way up to the control room.

Inside the control room, the Syndicate's devices were set up to interfere with the communications systems. Alex and Samara quickly set to work, disabling the devices and restoring the communication systems to their normal state. They worked efficiently, knowing that time was of the essence.

As they worked, Samara found a blueprint of the communications tower with additional information about the Syndicate's plans. It revealed that the Syndicate intended to use the tower to broadcast a signal that would disrupt communication channels throughout the city.

"This blueprint gives us a lot of useful information," Samara said. "We need to make sure that the Syndicate's signal is completely shut down."

Alex agreed. They completed their work at the communications tower and made their way back to their car. Their next destination was a site indicated on the blueprints as a testing facility. This facility was where the Syndicate was planning to test their technology on a larger scale.

The testing facility was located in an industrial area outside the city. The building was heavily guarded, with security cameras and patrols around the perimeter. Alex and Samara had to be cautious as they approached.

They observed the facility from a distance, noting the guards' patterns and the location of security cameras. Alex identified a potential entry point—a ventilation shaft that led into the building. They used their tools to gain access and climbed into the facility.

Inside, the testing facility was filled with advanced technology and equipment. The Syndicate's devices were being prepared for their next phase of deployment. Alex and Samara moved through the facility, avoiding detection and searching for key areas to sabotage.

They found the main control room where the Syndicate's devices were being monitored and prepared. The room was filled with screens displaying various data and activity logs. Alex and Samara quickly set to work, disabling the devices and ensuring that they could not be activated.

While working, Alex discovered a hidden compartment in one of the control panels. Inside, he found documents detailing the Syndicate's plans for a massive deployment of their technology. The documents included information about several key sites where the technology would be used to create widespread disruptions.

"This is crucial information," Alex said, examining the documents. "We need to take these with us and make sure that everyone knows about the Syndicate's plans."

Samara agreed, and they carefully gathered the documents and other important data. They finished their work at the testing facility and made their way back to their safehouse.

At the safehouse, Alex and Samara reviewed the documents and data they had collected. They found detailed plans for the Syndicate's technology deployment and identified key locations that needed immediate attention.

"We have to act quickly," Samara said. "If we can disrupt the Syndicate's plans at these locations, we might be able to prevent their technology from causing major problems."

Alex nodded. "We need to coordinate with our contacts and make sure that we have the resources to execute our plan. The city is depending on us."

They spent the night preparing for their final push against the Syndicate. They coordinated with law enforcement and other allies to ensure that they had the support they needed. Their plan was to target the remaining key locations and neutralize the Syndicate's technology before it could be deployed.

As dawn approached, Alex and Samara set out for the first location on their list. They knew that the success of their mission depended on their ability to act quickly and decisively. The city's safety was in their hands, and they were determined to see their plan through to the end.

Their journey was far from over, but Alex and Samara were ready to face whatever challenges lay ahead. They had come this far, and they were not going to stop until they had stopped the Syndicate and protected the city from their dangerous plans.

The Final Countdown

The sky was still dark when Alex and Samara set out for their next target. The information they had gathered from the Syndicate's testing facility had revealed several key locations where the Syndicate planned to deploy their technology. Their mission was clear: stop the Syndicate's plans before they could disrupt the city.

Their first stop was an abandoned warehouse on the edge of town. According to their intel, this was one of the main sites where the Syndicate was preparing their technology for deployment. The warehouse was large and isolated, making it an ideal location for their operations.

Alex and Samara arrived at the warehouse just as the sun was beginning to rise. They parked their car a safe distance away and approached on foot. The warehouse was surrounded by a high fence topped with barbed wire. There were guards patrolling the perimeter, and the area was heavily secured.

"We need to find a way inside without being seen," Samara said, scanning the area for possible entry points.

Alex spotted a small service door on the side of the warehouse that looked less guarded. They approached the door carefully, making sure to stay out of sight. Alex examined the lock and used his tools to pick it open. They slipped inside the warehouse, grateful for the cover of the shadows.

The inside of the warehouse was dimly lit and filled with crates and equipment. The Syndicate's technology was scattered around the room, with several devices in various stages of assembly. Alex and Samara knew they needed to act quickly to prevent the devices from being activated.

They moved through the warehouse, avoiding the guards who were patrolling the area. Samara used her knowledge of security systems to disable the alarms and cameras, making it easier for them to navigate the space.

As they reached the main assembly area, Alex noticed a control panel connected to the devices. He approached it and began examining the setup. The panel was set to activate the devices on a timer, and it looked like the Syndicate was planning to deploy their technology within hours.

"This panel controls the devices," Alex said, pointing to the control panel. "We need to disable it before it's too late."

Samara nodded and began working on the control panel. She used her tools to carefully dismantle the connections and override the timer settings. Alex continued to secure the devices, making sure they could not be activated.

Just as they were finishing up, they heard footsteps approaching. Alex and Samara quickly hid behind a stack of crates, holding their breath as the guards walked by. The guards were talking about the upcoming deployment and seemed unaware of the intruders.

Once the guards had passed, Alex and Samara resumed their work. They finished disabling the control panel and moved to the next area of the warehouse, where additional devices were being stored.

They found several more devices ready for deployment, but they were not yet activated. Alex and Samara carefully disarmed the devices and made sure they could not be used.

With their work in the warehouse complete, Alex and Samara left the building and made their way to their next location—a facility on the outskirts of the city that was critical to the Syndicate's plans. This facility was used to monitor and control the deployment of their technology across multiple sites.

The facility was a modern building with heavy security. There were guards at every entrance, and the building was equipped with advanced surveillance systems. Alex and Samara knew they needed a different approach to get inside.

They found a small maintenance access point on the side of the building. Using their tools, they managed to bypass the security and enter the facility. Inside, they navigated through a series of hallways and offices until they reached the central control room.

The control room was filled with screens and control panels, monitoring the Syndicate's technology across the city. Alex and Samara approached the main console, where they could see real-time data and maps showing the locations of the devices.

"This is where they're managing everything," Samara said, pointing to the screens. "If we can disrupt their control systems here, we might be able to prevent them from coordinating their deployment."

Alex nodded and began working on the console. He used his skills to access the control systems and disrupt the data feeds. Samara helped by disabling additional security measures and ensuring that their actions did not trigger alarms.

As they worked, they discovered a scheduled transmission that was set to activate the Syndicate's devices across the city. The transmission was set to occur within the next hour, and they realized they had to act quickly to stop it.

"We need to shut down this transmission," Alex said, working to override the scheduled activation. "If we can stop this signal, it will prevent the Syndicate from deploying their technology."

Samara monitored the systems and provided assistance as Alex worked on disabling the transmission. It was a tense and complex process, but they managed to break the link between the control room and the devices.

With the transmission disabled, Alex and Samara prepared to leave the facility. They retraced their steps, carefully avoiding the guards and security cameras. As they exited the building, they could see the city waking up, unaware of the crisis that had been averted.

Their next destination was a central hub where the Syndicate planned to deploy their technology on a large scale. This hub was located in a heavily fortified area, and it would be their most challenging target yet.

Alex and Samara approached the hub under the cover of darkness, using their knowledge of the facility's layout to find a way inside. They managed to bypass the security and enter the building, making their way to the main control center.

The control center was a high-tech room filled with monitors and equipment. The Syndicate's technology was being prepared for deployment, and the room was bustling with activity. Alex and Samara knew they had to act fast.

They began disabling the devices and disrupting the control systems. Samara used her skills to access the central computer and override the deployment schedules. Alex focused on dismantling the equipment and ensuring that the technology could not be used.

As they worked, they encountered several guards and technicians. They had to use all their skills to avoid detection and complete their mission. Despite the challenges, they managed to secure the control center and prevent the Syndicate from deploying their technology.

With their work complete, Alex and Samara left the hub and headed back to their safehouse. They were exhausted but relieved to have stopped the Syndicate's plans. The city was safe for now, but they knew that their work was not over.

They reviewed their actions and made plans for any further steps needed to secure the city and prevent future threats. Alex and Samara had faced many challenges and dangers, but their determination and teamwork had seen them through.

As they prepared for the next phase of their mission, they reflected on their journey and the obstacles they had overcome. They were ready to face whatever lay ahead and ensure that the Syndicate's plans were thwarted.

Their adventure was far from over, but Alex and Samara were committed to protecting the city and stopping any threats that came their way. They had proven their courage and skills, and they were ready for whatever challenges lay ahead.

Secrets Beneath the Surface

The sun was setting, casting long shadows across the city. Alex and Samara had been working tirelessly to stop the Syndicate's plans. Their next challenge was uncovering a hidden facility that had just come to light. The information they had gathered indicated that this facility held the key to the Syndicate's ultimate weapon.

They met in their safehouse to discuss their next steps. The blueprints and documents they had found revealed that the hidden facility was located underground, beneath an old, abandoned subway station. This station had long been forgotten by most people, making it an ideal place for the Syndicate to hide their most critical operations.

"We need to find out what's down there," Samara said, examining the map. "The Syndicate's plans might be more dangerous than we thought."

Alex nodded. "We should be prepared for anything. Let's gather our equipment and head out."

They packed their gear and set off towards the old subway station. The area around it was rundown and deserted, adding to the feeling of isolation. The entrance to the subway station was concealed behind a thick layer of dirt and debris. They had to clear a path to reveal the rusty metal door.

Using a crowbar, Alex pried open the door, revealing a dark staircase leading down into the depths. They descended cautiously, using their flashlights to illuminate the way. The air was cold and damp, and the walls of the staircase were lined with old, peeling tiles.

At the bottom of the stairs, they found themselves in a large, cavernous space. The old subway station had been repurposed into a high-tech facility, with rows of computers and machinery filling the space. The Syndicate's operations were clearly in full swing.

Alex and Samara moved stealthily through the facility, trying to avoid detection. They noticed that the facility was equipped with security cameras and guards. Their task was to find the main control room and gather as much information as possible.

As they made their way through the facility, they encountered a network of corridors and rooms, each filled with complex equipment and high-tech devices. The facility was a maze, and it was easy to get disoriented.

They followed the map they had found to navigate through the labyrinth. Each corner they turned brought them closer to their goal, but also increased the risk of being discovered. Samara used her skills to disable security cameras and alarms, ensuring they could move more freely.

After what felt like hours of navigating the facility, they finally reached the control room. The door was locked, but Alex quickly picked the lock and they entered. The control room was filled with screens and terminals, displaying information about the Syndicate's operations.

"This is it," Alex said, looking at the array of monitors. "We need to find out what they're planning and how we can stop it."

Samara began examining the terminals, searching for any data related to the Syndicate's plans. She found several files and documents detailing the development of a new type of weapon. The weapon was designed to cause widespread chaos and destruction, and the Syndicate was preparing to deploy it across the city.

"We've got to stop this," Samara said, her voice filled with urgency. "If they activate this weapon, it could cause massive damage."

Alex agreed. "We need to find out where they're storing the weapon and how we can neutralize it."

They continued to search the control room and found a secure vault where the weapon was being stored. The vault was protected by advanced security measures, including biometric scanners and reinforced steel doors.

Alex used his skills to bypass the security and open the vault. Inside, they found the weapon—an intricate device with several layers of protection. It was clear that this weapon was not just any ordinary piece of technology; it was designed to be extremely dangerous.

As they examined the weapon, they discovered a series of activation codes and triggers. The weapon could be deployed remotely, making it even more dangerous. Samara took notes on the activation codes and began working on disabling the weapon's mechanisms.

Alex kept watch, ensuring that no one would interrupt their work. The facility was still heavily guarded, and they had to be vigilant to avoid detection. They knew that if they were caught, their mission could be compromised.

After hours of careful work, Samara managed to disable the weapon's activation system. The device was no longer a threat, but they still needed to find a way to prevent it from being used in the future.

They collected as much information as they could from the control room, including data on the Syndicate's plans and the locations of other facilities. With their mission in the facility complete, they prepared to leave.

As they made their way back through the facility, they encountered a group of guards who were on high alert. Alex and Samara had to use all their skills to evade capture. They moved quickly and silently, taking advantage of the shadows to avoid detection.

Eventually, they reached the exit and emerged back into the old subway station. They were relieved to be out of the facility, but their work was far from over. They still needed to ensure that the information they had gathered was shared with the authorities and that the Syndicate's plans were stopped once and for all.

They made their way back to their safehouse and began organizing the information they had collected. They contacted their allies and shared the details of the Syndicate's operations, ensuring that the right people were informed.

As they worked, they reflected on their journey and the challenges they had faced. They had uncovered dangerous plans and thwarted a major threat, but they knew that their mission was not yet complete.

The city was safe for now, but they were aware that the Syndicate might still have other plans in the works. They prepared for any further challenges and continued to stay vigilant.

Their adventure had been filled with mystery, danger, and discovery, and they were ready for whatever lay ahead. Alex and Samara had proven their courage and skill, and they were determined to see their mission through to the end.

The Hidden Vault

The sky was clear as Alex and Samara drove towards their next destination: an old mansion on the outskirts of the city. They had uncovered new information that suggested the Syndicate had hidden a crucial piece of their operation there. This mansion was rumored to be a former hideout, and its location was linked to a secret vault where they might find more evidence about the Syndicate's plans.

As they arrived at the mansion, they saw that it was in a state of decay. The mansion had once been grand, but now it looked abandoned, with broken windows and overgrown vines covering the walls. It was clear that no one had been here for a long time.

"This place looks like it's been empty for years," Samara said, examining the outside. "But the information we have points to this being the key location."

Alex nodded. "We need to be careful. The Syndicate might have left traps or hidden security here."

They parked their car a little distance away and approached the mansion on foot. The front entrance was boarded up, but they found a side door that was slightly ajar. Alex pushed the door open, and they stepped inside.

The interior of the mansion was even more dilapidated than the outside. Dust covered everything, and the air was thick with the smell of mildew. The

THE HIDDEN VAULT

grand chandelier hanging from the ceiling was covered in cobwebs, and the once opulent furniture was now faded and broken.

Alex and Samara used their flashlights to explore the mansion. They moved cautiously through the dark hallways, keeping an eye out for any signs of recent activity or hidden dangers.

After searching through several rooms, they found a library filled with old books and documents. The library had a large fireplace with a hidden compartment behind it. Samara noticed the compartment and carefully opened it, revealing a set of old keys and a dusty journal.

"This might be important," Samara said, holding up the journal. "Let's see what it says."

Alex took the keys and examined them. They looked old but seemed to be in good condition. Samara opened the journal and began reading aloud.

The journal was written in neat handwriting and detailed the history of the mansion. It mentioned a hidden vault that was used to store valuable items and documents. The vault was said to be located in the basement, concealed behind a series of hidden doors and passages.

"The vault should be down in the basement," Samara said, looking at the journal. "We need to find the entrance."

They made their way to the basement stairs and descended into the darkness. The basement was cold and damp, with old storage rooms and boxes scattered around. They searched through the basement, looking for any sign of the hidden vault.

After some searching, Alex found a hidden door behind a large stack of crates. The door was covered in dust and grime, but it seemed to lead to another part of the basement. Using the old keys, he unlocked the door and pushed it open.

Inside, they found a narrow passageway that led further down. The passage was lined with old stone walls and had a musty smell. They followed the passage, their footsteps echoing in the silence.

At the end of the passage, they came to a large, heavy door with a complex lock. The door was old and ornate, with intricate carvings and a metal plate in the center. The lock looked challenging, but Alex was determined to get it open.

He took out his tools and began working on the lock. It was a tricky process, and it took some time, but eventually, the lock clicked open. The door creaked as Alex and Samara pushed it open, revealing the hidden vault.

The vault was a large room filled with old crates, documents, and other items. The walls were lined with shelves holding various objects, and in the center of the room was a large table covered in papers and files.

Alex and Samara entered the vault and began examining the contents. They found a collection of documents that detailed the Syndicate's operations, including plans for future attacks and information about their hidden assets.

"This is it," Alex said, looking at the papers. "We've found the heart of their operation."

Samara nodded and began sorting through the documents. She found several files related to the Syndicate's plans for a new type of weapon, along with instructions for its deployment. There were also maps and diagrams showing the locations of various targets.

As they reviewed the documents, they realized that the Syndicate's plans were more extensive and dangerous than they had initially thought. The new weapon was designed to cause widespread destruction, and the Syndicate had already begun preparations for its deployment.

"We need to get this information out," Samara said. "The authorities need to know what's coming."

Alex agreed. "We should contact our allies and make sure this information gets to the right people. We also need to find a way to neutralize the weapon before it's too late."

They collected the documents and prepared to leave the vault. As they were about to exit, they heard a noise coming from the basement. It sounded like footsteps and voices.

"They must have found out we're here," Alex said, his voice low. "We need to move quickly."

They hurried back through the passage and up the basement stairs. The mansion was still quiet, but they knew they had to be careful. They made their way to the side door and exited the mansion, being as discreet as possible.

Once outside, they made their way back to their car. They were relieved to have escaped the mansion and were eager to get the information to their allies. They drove back to the city, their minds racing with the implications of what they had uncovered.

When they arrived at their safehouse, they immediately contacted their contacts and shared the details of the Syndicate's plans. The authorities were alerted, and preparations were made to prevent the Syndicate from carrying out their attacks.

Alex and Samara knew that their work was not yet done. They had uncovered a major part of the Syndicate's operation, but there was still more to be done to ensure the safety of the city. They continued to work tirelessly, analyzing the information and planning their next steps.

Their mission had been filled with challenges and dangers, but they were determined to see it through to the end. They had proven their courage and resourcefulness, and they were ready to face whatever lay ahead.

As they prepared for the next phase of their mission, Alex and Samara reflected on their journey and the obstacles they had overcome. They were committed to protecting the city and stopping any threats that came their way. Their adventure was far from over, but they were ready for whatever challenges lay ahead.

The Final Countdown

The city was on edge. Alex and Samara had just uncovered a major piece of the Syndicate's plans, but they knew the real challenge lay ahead. The Syndicate was about to launch a devastating weapon, and they had to stop it before it was too late.

They had gathered all the information they could from the hidden vault. The Syndicate's plans were clear: they intended to activate their weapon within the next 24 hours, causing chaos and destruction across the city. Alex and Samara knew they had to act fast.

The first step was to locate the weapon's activation site. According to the documents, the weapon would be triggered from a remote location, hidden somewhere in the city. They needed to find this location and neutralize the weapon before the countdown reached zero.

Alex and Samara spent the night analyzing the maps and documents they had recovered. They looked for any clues that might indicate the weapon's location. They cross-referenced the data with known locations and came up with a list of possible sites.

By early morning, they had narrowed down their search to a warehouse on the edge of the city. The warehouse was an old building used for storage and had been abandoned for years. It matched the description of the kind of place the Syndicate would use for their operation.

They decided to check it out. The warehouse was situated in a desolate area, surrounded by tall fences and overgrown vegetation. It looked like a perfect hiding spot. Alex and Samara approached the warehouse carefully, keeping an eye out for any signs of activity.

As they neared the entrance, they saw that the doors were partially open. Alex led the way, cautiously pushing the doors further apart. The inside of the warehouse was dark and filled with dust. Old crates and barrels were scattered around, and the air smelled of damp and decay.

They used their flashlights to navigate through the warehouse, moving quietly and avoiding any obstacles. They searched for any sign of the weapon or its activation system. The warehouse was large, and it took them a while to explore each corner.

In the back of the warehouse, they found a large, locked door. The door was reinforced with metal and had a complex lock. It looked like it could be hiding something important.

Alex took out his tools and began working on the lock. It was a challenging task, and it took him several minutes to get it open. When the lock finally clicked, he pushed the door open, revealing a hidden room.

The hidden room was filled with high-tech equipment and computers. In the center of the room was a large control panel with several screens and buttons. It was clear that this was where the weapon was being controlled.

Samara approached the control panel and began examining it. She found a series of activation codes and a countdown timer. The timer was set for less than 12 hours, indicating that the weapon was close to being activated.

"We need to stop this now," Samara said, her voice filled with urgency. "If we don't, the weapon will be deployed."

Alex nodded and began working on the control panel. He tried to bypass the security systems and disable the activation codes. It was a difficult task, and he had to work quickly to avoid triggering any alarms.

As Alex worked, Samara kept watch for any signs of intruders. The warehouse was still quiet, but they knew the Syndicate might send reinforcements at any moment. They had to finish their work before it was too late.

After several tense minutes, Alex managed to disable the control panel's security systems. He worked on the activation codes and successfully blocked the weapon from being triggered. The countdown timer stopped, and the threat was temporarily neutralized.

"We've done it," Alex said, breathing a sigh of relief. "The weapon won't be activated as long as this control panel stays offline."

Samara nodded, but her expression remained serious. "We still need to make sure the Syndicate can't reactivate it. We should destroy the control panel and all the equipment here."

They gathered explosives from their gear and set them up around the control panel and the equipment. They placed the explosives carefully, making sure to target the critical components of the control panel.

With everything in place, they set the timer on the explosives and prepared to leave. The warehouse was about to be destroyed, and they needed to get to safety.

As they made their way out of the warehouse, they heard the sound of approaching vehicles. The Syndicate was coming. Alex and Samara hurried to their car and drove away from the warehouse, heading to a safe location where they could monitor the situation.

From a distance, they watched as the warehouse exploded in a massive fireball. The explosion sent debris flying, and the building was engulfed in flames. The control panel and the weapon were destroyed, ensuring that the Syndicate's plans were thwarted.

"We did it," Samara said, watching the flames. "The weapon is destroyed, and the threat is over."

Alex nodded, but he knew that their mission was far from over. The Syndicate was still out there, and they needed to continue their efforts to dismantle their operation and bring those responsible to justice.

They returned to their safehouse and continued their work. They contacted their allies and shared the news about the successful neutralization of the weapon. They also provided information about the Syndicate's remaining operations and locations.

The authorities began investigating the Syndicate's remaining facilities and making arrests. Alex and Samara continued to support the efforts, providing critical information and helping to coordinate the operations.

As the days went by, the city slowly returned to normal. The threat of the Syndicate's weapon was gone, and the people felt a sense of relief. Alex and Samara had played a crucial role in stopping the Syndicate and protecting the city.

Their journey had been filled with danger and challenges, but they had proven their bravery and determination. They had faced their fears and overcome obstacles, and they were ready for whatever came next.

As they looked out over the city, they felt a sense of accomplishment. They had made a difference and had helped keep the city safe. Their adventure was far from over, but they were prepared to face whatever challenges lay ahead.

The Shadow's Secret

The morning sun was just beginning to rise over the city when Alex and Samara received a mysterious message. The message was brief and cryptic, saying only: "The Shadow knows more. Meet me where the old clock tower stands." There was no signature, only the words.

"Who could it be?" Samara wondered aloud, staring at the message on her phone.

"I don't know," Alex replied, "but it sounds like someone who knows more about the Syndicate's plans. We should check it out."

The old clock tower was a historic landmark in the city, a tall and weathered building with a clock face that had long stopped working. It stood in a quiet park, surrounded by overgrown grass and trees. Once a symbol of the city's past, it was now a forgotten relic.

Alex and Samara drove to the park where the clock tower stood. The sun was still low in the sky, casting long shadows across the ground. They parked their car at the edge of the park and walked towards the clock tower.

As they approached, they noticed that the area was deserted. The old clock tower loomed ahead, its face cracked and its hands frozen in time. The park was silent, save for the distant chirping of birds.

"This place feels eerie," Samara said, looking around. "I hope this isn't a trap."

Alex nodded, feeling the same sense of unease. "Let's be cautious. We don't know who we're meeting or what to expect."

They reached the base of the clock tower and found a small, hidden entrance. The door was slightly ajar, as if someone had left it open. Alex carefully pushed the door open and they stepped inside.

The interior of the clock tower was dark and dusty. The air was cool and musty, with the smell of old wood and stone. They climbed a creaky staircase that spiraled upwards, leading to the top of the tower. The steps were uneven and worn, but they made their way slowly, listening for any signs of movement.

At the top of the tower, they found a small room with a large, broken clock mechanism. The room was filled with old gears and machinery, and the clock face was cracked and covered in grime. In the center of the room was a figure standing in the shadows.

"Who's there?" Alex called out, his voice echoing in the empty space.

The figure stepped into the light. It was a man in his late fifties, with a weathered face and piercing blue eyes. He wore a long coat and a fedora hat, which cast a shadow over his face. The man looked at them with a serious expression.

"I'm the Shadow," the man said in a low voice. "I have information that could help you. But first, you need to prove your trustworthiness."

Alex and Samara exchanged wary glances. "What do you want us to do?" Alex asked.

"The Syndicate has a hidden base in the city," the Shadow explained. "It's well protected and heavily guarded. I have the location, but I need you to verify it for me. If you can confirm the location and gather any evidence, I'll give you the full details."

"Why should we trust you?" Samara asked. "How do we know you're not working with the Syndicate?"

The Shadow's eyes narrowed. "I have my reasons for wanting to stop them. I've been tracking their activities for years. I know they are planning something big, and it's in everyone's interest to see them brought down."

Alex and Samara considered the Shadow's words. They had little choice but to trust him, as they needed more information to defeat the Syndicate.

"Alright," Alex said. "We'll check out the location. What's the address?"

The Shadow handed Alex a folded piece of paper with the address written on it. "Be careful. The Syndicate won't make it easy for you."

With the address in hand, Alex and Samara left the clock tower and headed to their car. They drove to the location, which turned out to be an old, abandoned factory on the outskirts of the city.

The factory was a large, derelict building with broken windows and a rusted metal exterior. It looked like it hadn't been used in years. The area around it was desolate, with only a few stray dogs wandering the streets.

"This is the place," Samara said as they arrived. "Let's see if there's any activity inside."

They parked their car a safe distance away and approached the factory on foot. The front entrance was blocked by a rusty gate, but they found a side door that was slightly open.

Alex and Samara slipped inside, moving quietly through the dark and empty building. The factory was vast, with tall ceilings and rows of old machinery covered in dust. They used their flashlights to navigate through the shadows, searching for any signs of the Syndicate.

As they explored the factory, they found evidence of recent activity. There were fresh footprints in the dust and a few scattered papers that looked like they had been used recently. They followed the trail of evidence to a hidden door at the back of the factory.

The door was secured with a heavy lock, but Alex managed to pick it open. Inside, they found a small room filled with equipment and documents. The room was clearly being used for planning and coordination, with maps and files scattered around.

"This must be it," Alex said, examining the documents. "The Syndicate's operations center."

Samara looked through the files and found several papers detailing their plans. There were maps showing target locations, diagrams of their weapon systems, and lists of names. It was clear that the Syndicate was preparing for something significant.

"This is valuable information," Samara said. "We need to take it back and analyze it."

Suddenly, they heard the sound of footsteps approaching. Alex and Samara quickly gathered the documents and prepared to leave. They needed to escape before they were discovered.

They slipped out of the room and made their way back to the side door. As they were about to exit, they saw a group of Syndicate operatives entering the factory. The operatives were armed and looked alert.

Alex and Samara moved stealthily, avoiding detection as they made their way to their car. They managed to slip out of the factory and drive away before the operatives noticed them.

Back at their safehouse, they reviewed the documents they had recovered. The information was extensive and revealed the Syndicate's plans for a major operation. They had detailed the deployment of their weapon systems and outlined their targets.

"This is crucial," Alex said. "We need to get this information to the authorities and stop the Syndicate's plans."

They contacted their allies and shared the details of the Syndicate's operation. The authorities began mobilizing to prevent the attacks and take down the Syndicate's remaining facilities.

Alex and Samara knew that the fight was not over. The Syndicate was still a threat, and they needed to remain vigilant. They continued to work with their allies, tracking the Syndicate's movements and uncovering additional information.

Their mission had taken them through danger and intrigue, but they were determined to see it through to the end. They had faced challenges and uncovered secrets, and they were ready for whatever came next.

As they prepared for the final stages of their mission, Alex and Samara reflected on their journey. They had proven their bravery and resourcefulness, and they were committed to protecting the city and stopping the Syndicate.

Their adventure was far from over, but they were prepared for the challenges that lay ahead. With their determination and courage, they were ready to confront the Syndicate and ensure that their plans were stopped once and for all.

The Hidden Agenda

Alex and Samara were still dealing with the shock of the Syndicate's operation. The information they had uncovered was overwhelming, but they knew they couldn't stop now. The Syndicate was planning something big, and they needed to find out what it was before it was too late.

They had managed to gather a lot of useful information from the factory, but there were still many unanswered questions. They needed to figure out the full extent of the Syndicate's plans and stop them before it was too late.

Late that night, they sat in their safehouse, surrounded by maps, documents, and files. They spread everything out on the table, trying to piece together the puzzle. Their eyes were tired, but their determination was strong.

"Look at this," Samara said, pointing to one of the maps. "There's something here that doesn't make sense."

Alex leaned in to examine the map. It showed several locations marked with red Xs, but one of the locations seemed different. It was marked with a series of numbers and letters that didn't match the other locations.

"This must be important," Alex said. "It could be the key to understanding their plan."

They decided to investigate the mysterious location. The address on the map led them to a nondescript building on the outskirts of the city. It was a small, unremarkable warehouse that seemed ordinary at first glance.

As they arrived, they noticed that the warehouse was heavily guarded. There were security cameras, guard posts, and a tall fence surrounding the property. It was clear that the Syndicate was taking extra precautions.

"We'll have to be careful," Samara said. "We can't just walk in there."

They parked their car at a distance and observed the warehouse. They noticed that the guards followed a regular patrol pattern, and there was a small side entrance that looked less guarded.

"We should use that entrance," Alex suggested. "It might be our best chance to get inside."

They waited until the guards were on the other side of the warehouse and made their move. They slipped through the side entrance and into the warehouse. The interior was dimly lit and filled with rows of crates and boxes. The air was thick with dust and the smell of old wood.

They moved quietly through the warehouse, avoiding any noise that might alert the guards. They followed a series of hallways and finally arrived at a large room at the back of the building. The room was filled with high-tech equipment and computers, similar to what they had seen in the factory.

"This must be another operations center," Samara said, looking around. "We need to find out what they're planning here."

They began searching through the documents and files scattered around the room. The papers contained detailed plans for various operations, but one document stood out. It was a list of locations with specific dates and times.

"This looks like a schedule," Alex said. "It could be a timeline for their attacks."

They examined the list closely and noticed that the dates and times corresponded with the locations marked on the map they had found earlier. It seemed like the Syndicate was planning a series of coordinated attacks across the city.

"We need to stop this," Samara said. "If we can get this information to the authorities, they can prevent the attacks."

As they prepared to leave, they heard the sound of footsteps approaching. The guards were coming closer. Alex and Samara quickly gathered the documents and moved to hide behind some crates.

The guards entered the room, talking in low voices. They seemed to be discussing the security measures and the schedule for their operations. Alex and Samara waited silently, holding their breath.

Once the guards left, Alex and Samara made their way back to the side entrance. They slipped out of the warehouse and hurried to their car. They drove back to their safehouse, anxious to review the information they had collected.

Back at the safehouse, they analyzed the documents and confirmed their fears. The Syndicate was planning multiple attacks across the city, targeting key infrastructure and public places. The attacks were scheduled to occur over the next few days, causing maximum chaos and disruption.

"This is worse than we thought," Alex said. "We need to alert the authorities immediately."

They contacted their contacts in law enforcement and shared the details of the Syndicate's plan. The authorities began mobilizing to prevent the attacks, setting up security measures and increasing patrols in the targeted areas.

Alex and Samara continued to assist in the efforts, providing critical information and coordinating with the authorities. They knew that time was running out, and every minute counted.

As the days went by, the city was on high alert. The authorities worked tirelessly to thwart the Syndicate's plans, and Alex and Samara kept a close watch on the situation.

Despite their efforts, the Syndicate was relentless. They continued to move their operations and adapt their plans, trying to stay one step ahead of the authorities. Alex and Samara had to stay vigilant and adapt to the changing situation.

One night, as they were monitoring the situation, they received another message from the Shadow. It was another cryptic note that read: "The final piece is hidden where the shadows fall. Find it before it's too late."

"What does this mean?" Samara asked, puzzled.

"It sounds like a clue," Alex said. "We need to figure out where the shadows fall and what the final piece could be."

They reviewed the message and considered possible locations. The Shadow's clue seemed to suggest that the final piece of the Syndicate's plan was hidden in a place where shadows were prominent.

They thought about the city's landmarks and locations where shadows might fall. The old clock tower came to mind, with its tall structure and shadowy corners.

"We should check the clock tower again," Alex said. "It might be connected to the final piece of the Syndicate's plan."

They drove back to the clock tower and arrived late at night. The area was quiet and deserted, with only the distant sounds of the city in the background. They approached the clock tower cautiously, using their flashlights to navigate through the darkness.

As they reached the base of the tower, they noticed something unusual. There was a faint glow coming from one of the windows near the top of the tower. It was as if something was shining from inside.

"That's strange," Samara said. "There shouldn't be any light up there."

They climbed the stairs to the top of the clock tower and found the window with the glow. They carefully opened the window and peered inside. The light was coming from a small room at the top of the tower.

Inside the room, they saw a large, ornate box sitting in the center. The box was covered in intricate patterns and had a keyhole in the center. It looked ancient and valuable.

"This must be the final piece," Alex said. "We need to get that box."

They climbed through the window and carefully moved the box to a safe area. Alex examined the keyhole and found that it matched a key they had found earlier in the factory.

Using the key, Alex unlocked the box. Inside, they found a set of documents and a strange device. The documents detailed the Syndicate's final plan, including a list of key targets and instructions for deploying their weapon systems.

The device was a small, high-tech gadget that seemed to be a control unit for the Syndicate's operations. It was designed to remotely activate their weapon systems and coordinate their attacks.

"This is it," Samara said. "We've found the final piece of their plan."

Alex and Samara quickly gathered the documents and the device and made their way back to their car. They needed to get this information to the authorities and prevent the Syndicate from carrying out their final attacks.

As they drove to their safehouse, they felt a sense of urgency. The Syndicate's plans were coming to fruition, and they had to act fast to stop them.

Back at the safehouse, they contacted their allies and shared the information they had found. The authorities worked quickly to dismantle the Syndicate's remaining operations and prevent the final attacks.

The city remained on high alert as the authorities conducted raids and secured the targeted locations. Alex and Samara continued to support the efforts, providing crucial information and coordinating with law enforcement.

Despite the challenges, they had successfully thwarted the Syndicate's plans and prevented their final attacks. The city was safe once again, thanks to their bravery and determination.

As they looked back on their journey, Alex and Samara felt a sense of accomplishment. They had faced danger and intrigue, uncovered hidden agendas, and made a difference in the fight against the Syndicate.

Their adventure was far from over, but they were prepared for whatever challenges lay ahead. With their courage and resourcefulness, they were ready to confront the Syndicate and ensure that their plans were stopped once and for all.

Dawn of a New Era

The city, once shrouded in the dark threat of the Syndicate, had begun to breathe a sigh of relief. With their plans thwarted, the streets returned to their normal hustle and bustle, though the scars of their nefarious plot would linger for some time. Alex and Samara had become local heroes, though they remained humble, preferring to blend into the background rather than seek the spotlight.

Weeks had passed since the final showdown at the clock tower. The Syndicate's remaining operatives had been apprehended, and the authorities had dismantled their criminal network. The dangerous device and detailed documents they had uncovered had proven instrumental in bringing the organization to its knees.

As they walked through the park one sunny afternoon, Alex and Samara took a moment to reflect. The park was now vibrant and full of life, a stark contrast to the tension and fear that had gripped the city not long ago. Families enjoyed picnics, children played on swings, and the sound of laughter filled the air.

"It feels surreal," Samara said, watching a group of kids playing near the fountain. "It's hard to believe how much things have changed."

Alex nodded. "It's amazing how quickly things can turn around when people come together for a common cause."

They had been busy for weeks, working closely with the authorities to ensure that the remnants of the Syndicate's plans were fully dismantled. The city had held a ceremony to honor those who had contributed to the effort, and while Alex and Samara had declined the formal accolades, they had been deeply touched by the city's gratitude.

As they strolled through the park, Alex's phone buzzed. He glanced at the screen and saw a message from their contact in law enforcement.

"Looks like there's one more thing we need to take care of," Alex said, showing Samara the message. "There's been a lead on some remaining Syndicate assets. We should check it out."

They made their way to the location mentioned in the message—a warehouse on the outskirts of town. It was a quiet, unassuming place, but the message indicated that it might hold some important information.

Inside the warehouse, they found a few remaining documents and some scattered files. These seemed to be leftover materials from the Syndicate's operations, but nothing that posed an immediate threat. As they gathered the documents, they found a note tucked inside one of the files.

The note was brief but intriguing. It read: "The Syndicate may be down, but the shadows always remain. Look beyond the surface, and you'll find the truth."

"What do you think this means?" Samara asked, examining the note.

"It sounds like a cryptic message," Alex replied. "It could be a reminder that while the Syndicate's plans have been stopped, there may still be hidden threats out there."

They decided to keep the note for further investigation. For now, their immediate concern was wrapping up their work and ensuring the city was secure.

Back at their safehouse, they reviewed the remaining documents and found nothing that required immediate action. The city was recovering, and people were slowly returning to their normal lives. The authorities continued to monitor for any lingering threats, and Alex and Samara remained vigilant.

One evening, as they sat on the balcony of their safehouse, they looked out over the city. The skyline was bathed in the warm glow of the setting sun, and the streets below were bustling with activity.

"We've done a lot," Samara said, her voice filled with satisfaction. "But I have a feeling there's always more to uncover."

Alex smiled. "That's what makes this job so interesting. There's always another mystery to solve, another adventure to embark on."

They sat in comfortable silence, enjoying the view and the peacefulness of the moment. The city was safe, and the immediate threat had been neutralized, but they knew their journey was far from over. There were always new challenges and mysteries waiting to be discovered.

As the sun dipped below the horizon, casting long shadows across the city, Alex and Samara felt a renewed sense of purpose. They were ready for whatever came next, prepared to face new adventures and confront hidden dangers.

With the city in their rearview mirror, they set out on their next mission, knowing that their fight for justice and truth was far from over. The shadows of the past may linger, but with their courage and determination, they were ready to shine a light on whatever lay ahead.

And so, their story continued, a testament to their bravery and resilience in the face of darkness. They embraced the future with hope and anticipation, ready to uncover new mysteries and ensure that the world remained a safer place for all.